PYTHONS

by Lucia Raatma

Children's Press®

An Imprint of Scholastic Inc.
New York   Toronto   London   Auckland   Sydney
Mexico City   New Delhi   Hong Kong
Danbury, Connecticut

Content Consultant
Dr. Stephen S. Ditchkoff
Professor of Wildlife
Auburn University
Auburn, Alabama

Photographs 2013: age fotostock: 27 (Chris Mattison/FLPA), 4,
5 background, 12 (Gerard Lacz); Alamy Images: 23 (blickwinkel/
Schmidbauer), 20 (Don Fuchs/LOOK Die Bildagentur der Fotografen
GmbH), 19 (H. Reinhard/Arco Images), 28 (Mary Evans Picture
Library); AP Images: 40 (Anthony Devlin), 36 (Tiffany Tompkins-
Condie/The Herald); Bob Italiano: 44 foreground, 45 foreground;
Dreamstime: cover (Johnbell), 15 (Mgkuijpers), 2 background, 3
background, 44 background, 45 background (Richard Sheppard);
Getty Images: 35 (Bay Ismoyo/AFP), 7 (E.R. Degginger/Photo
Researchers), 5 top, 11 (Joe McDonald/Visuals Unlimited);
iStockphoto/Mark Kostich: 39; National Geographic Stock/
Rich Reid: 5 bottom, 8; Newscom/David Brewster/MCT:
31; Shutterstock, Inc./Vishnevskiy Vasily: 1, 2 foreground, 3
foreground, 46; Superstock, Inc.: 16 (Animals Animals), 32
(Minden Pictures), 24 (NHPA).

Library of Congress Cataloging-in-Publication Data
Raatma, Lucia.
  Pythons/by Lucia Raatma.
    p. cm.–(Nature's children)
  Includes bibliographical references and index.
  ISBN-13: 978-0-531-26837-7 (lib. bdg.)
  ISBN-13: 978-0-531-25482-0 (pbk.)
  1. Pythons–Juvenile literature. I. Title.
  QL666.O67R33 2013
  597.96'78–dc23   2012000637

All rights reserved. Published in 2013 by Children's Press, an imprint
of Scholastic Inc.
Printed in China 62
SCHOLASTIC, CHILDREN'S PRESS, and associated logos are
trademarks and/or registered trademarks of Scholastic Inc.

1 2 3 4 5 6 7 8 9 10 R 22 21 20 19 18 17 16 15 14 13

Pythons

Class	Reptilia
Order	Squamata
Family	Pythonidae
Genus	Some scientists divide pythons into four genera; others use eight genera
Species	About 28 species
World distribution	Africa, the Pacific Islands, South and Southeast Asia, and Australia
Habitats	Primarily found in warm regions, including grasslands, rain forests, jungles, woodlands, and swamps
Distinctive physical characteristics	Certain species are among the largest of snakes; some grow to be as long as 30 feet (9 meters); some have distinct patterns and markings along their bodies; others are solid colors
Habits	They are constrictors that wrap around their prey; like all snakes, they swallow prey whole; they are good climbers and swimmers
Diet	Birds, small mammals, amphibians, and reptiles

PYTHONS

Contents

CHAPTER 1

All About Pythons

Pythons are among the largest, most powerful snakes in the world. They lack the poisonous bite that many snakes are famous for, but that doesn't make them any less deadly. These **constrictors** wrap their long, muscular bodies around their **prey** and squeeze until the unlucky animal can no longer breathe.

The **reticulated** python is the longest snake in the world. It can be as long as 32 feet (9.8 m). Most are about 20 feet (6 m) in length. These huge snakes can weigh up to 250 pounds (113 kilograms). That is more than an average adult man. Even the smallest python **species**, such as the pygmy python, grow to be about 2 feet (61 centimeters) long.

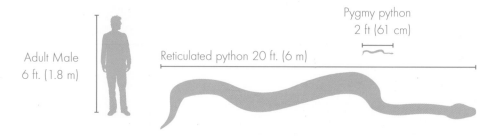

Pygmy python
2 ft (61 cm)

Adult Male
6 ft. (1.8 m)

Reticulated python 20 ft. (6 m)

Pythons are known for their incredible strength.

Python Basics

Like other snakes, pythons are covered with scales. They have an outer layer of skin on top of their scales. They shed this skin many times to make room for growth as their bodies get larger. Usually they shed their outer layer of skin all at once. The python rubs against a rock or other rough object when its old skin starts to get loose. Then it slithers out, leaving a complete outer layer of skin behind.

Pythons do not have ears, so they cannot hear. Instead, they feel vibrations in the air through their jawbones. Most have good eyesight, and their pupils dilate at night so they can see well in the dark. Pythons have thin tongues that they use to taste scents in the air instead of sniffing smells the way people or other animals do. Pythons do not have eyelids. Instead, they have clear scales that cover their eyes. As a result, they often seem to stare without blinking.

The tongue is an important sensory organ for pythons.

Colorful Creatures

Different python species can easily be identified by the colors and patterns of their scales. These features help each type of python blend in with its surroundings and stay hidden from prey.

The black-headed python has a dark black head and neck. The rest of its body has a wavy pattern of brown and tan that helps it blend in with the sandy, rocky areas of northern Australia. It is usually between 5 and 10 feet (1.5 and 3 m) long.

Indian pythons live in the forests and woodlands of India. These snakes have gray or tan bodies with brown patches outlined in yellow. This allows them to hide in the leaves and undergrowth of the forest floor. They can sometimes grow to more than 20 feet (6 m) long, but they rarely grow longer than 12 feet (3.7 m).

The green tree python lives in the rain forests of New Guinea and the Pacific Islands. It has a bright green body with small white speckles. This snake spends nearly all its time in trees and can grow to be 5 feet (1.5 m) long.

The green tree python blends in with its leafy home.

CHAPTER 2

Snake Survival

Pythons are reptiles. Reptiles are **cold-blooded** animals that crawl along the ground or walk on short legs. Because pythons are cold-blooded, their body temperature changes depending on the weather. If they are too cold, pythons might lie on a rock and bask in the sun. If they are too hot, they hide in the shade.

Pythons may hiss loudly when they feel threatened. They may also hide in logs, between rocks, or in holes. The ball python coils into a tight ball when it is in danger. The green tree python loops itself over tree branches or hangs by its tail to blend in with its surroundings. It bares its sharp teeth when startled.

FUN FACT! Green tree pythons have been known to strike out at birds as they fly past.

Lying on warm rocks can help a python keep its body temperature from getting too low.

Pythons and Their Prey

Pythons are fierce hunters. However, they do not need to chase after their meals. Instead, they hide and wait for unsuspecting prey to get close.

Most pythons have heat-sensing **pit organs** in their lips. These organs allow the snakes to detect any object or animal that is warmer than its surroundings. This helps pythons find prey even in total darkness.

Most pythons are active at night, from dusk until dawn. They often eat birds and small mammals. Some species also eat small reptiles and amphibians. The reticulated python has been known to eat animals as large as deer and pigs. The black-headed python sometimes eats other snakes. There have been rare cases in which pythons have eaten humans. However, pythons are not usually harmful to humans.

Pit organs enable pythons to sense even the smallest changes in temperature.

Massive Meals

Once a python senses nearby prey, it reaches out and grabs the animal's head with its teeth. It then wraps itself around the prey and begins squeezing. Most of a python's prey animals die from **suffocation**. Some die of heart failure. After the prey is dead, the python swallows it whole. Pythons have strong, flexible jaws that expand, so even large animals can fit inside their mouths.

After a python has swallowed its prey, it may take days or even weeks for the snake to **digest** its meal. The python's body expands to make enough room for the prey. The snake is usually inactive as it digests its food. It may not need to eat again for several weeks. Some pythons eat only four or five times a year.

FUN FACT! A python digests the entire body of its prey, except for fur or feathers.

Smaller prey such as mice are easy for pythons to swallow whole.

On Land and in Water

On the ground, pythons travel forward in straight lines. They use the muscles and scales on their bottom sides to pull themselves forward. Most pythons can travel only about 1 mile (1.6 kilometers) per hour on the ground. They don't need to move any faster because they wait for prey to come to them instead of chasing it down. Pythons can also climb trees. They use their prehensile tails to grip tree branches.

Some pythons live near bodies of water such as swamps and rivers. Burmese pythons are strong swimmers and can stay underwater for as long as 30 minutes. African rock pythons live on savannas, primarily along areas of rock. They, too, are good swimmers. This enables them to feed on ducks and other waterbirds.

Pythons can hang from trees to wait for prey to pass underneath them.

Dangerous Enemies

Most pythons are so powerful that they have few **predators** in the wild. However, some animals are still a danger to pythons. Dingoes, which are found in Australia, sometimes hunt black-headed pythons. Crocodiles, leopards, hyenas, and eagles prey on other species. Young pythons face many dangers when left alone. They can be prey for birds and small mammals such as foxes. In most cases, pythons are able to protect themselves in their **habitat**. Other animals fear them and try to keep their distance.

Humans are one of the biggest threats to pythons. They hunt pythons for their skin and to sell them as pets. Humans also cause harm to the natural areas where pythons live.

FUN FACT! Pythons are most likely to be attacked when they become sluggish after eating.

Humans are the main predators of adult pythons.

CHAPTER 3

A Python's Life

Winter is a difficult time of year for pythons and many other animals. Many mammals **hibernate** during the winter months. This means they go into a deep sleep. Their bodies use less energy, so they do not need as much food to survive. This process helps them live through cold weather when there is little to eat.

Many pythons do something similar. Their method of saving energy during the winter is called **brumation**. It begins at the time of year when the weather starts to get colder. The snakes eat a lot of food before brumation and then eat very little once the process begins. Unlike some hibernating animals, snakes do not sleep through the entire brumation period. Instead, they slow down and are much less active.

Pythons find safe places to hide during brumation.

Caring for Eggs

Most pythons breed in the early part of the spring. After mating, a female produces a clutch of eggs. The eggs vary in size and number, depending on the species. Burmese pythons lay up to 100 eggs at a time. A black-headed python may have fewer than 12 eggs each season. Reticulated pythons average 20 to 50 eggs, and some very large reticulated pythons can lay as many as 100 eggs at a time.

A female python arranges her eggs in a pile after laying them. Then she wraps herself around the pile and begins twitching her muscles. This raises the air temperature around the eggs and keeps them warm. She remains wrapped around the clutch until the eggs hatch a few months later. The mother rarely eats during this time. She is very protective and scares off animals that attempt to disturb her eggs.

Python mothers must watch closely for predators trying to eat their eggs.

A Python's Life Begins

Young pythons use a special tooth called an egg tooth to break out of their shells. As soon as they hatch, their mother leaves the nest. The baby pythons are left to survive on their own. Pythons do not live in big groups or families. Most are solitary and keep to themselves.

Depending on the species, baby pythons can be up to 2 feet (61 cm) long when they are born. They grow very quickly, and usually shed their skin for the first time between seven and ten days after hatching. Many pythons double or triple in length before they turn one year old. They usually live for 20 to 30 years.

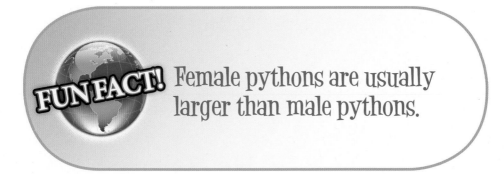

FUN FACT! Female pythons are usually larger than male pythons.

Newborn pythons look like tiny versions of their parents.

CHAPTER 4

Pythons Through the Ages

The word *python* comes from the name of a large serpent or dragon in ancient Greek mythology. In these stories, Python was created from mud after a huge flood. The creature lived in a mountain cave and frightened people living nearby. The god Apollo killed Python. This event was celebrated by the creation of the Pythian games. These games were races and contests of strength.

The ball python is also known as the royal python. This is because, according to stories, the Egyptian queen Cleopatra wore this type of python. She wrapped it around her wrist like a bracelet. Cleopatra is remembered for being beautiful and a powerful ruler.

In Greek mythology, the god Apollo killed a monster named Python.

Python Fossils

Snakes have existed for millions of years. Because snake bones are small and fragile, they have not left many fossils for scientists to study. Therefore, much of what is known about the history of snakes is based on ideas instead of hard facts. Scientists believe that most snake species are related to a type of ancient lizard that dug holes in the ground.

In October 2011, scientists in Germany discovered a python fossil that was about 15 million years old. The fossil shows just seven of the snake's vertebrae. They believe that the snake would have had 400 vertebrae when it was alive. Based on these findings, they believe that the python was about 11.5 feet (3.5 m) long.

FUN FACT! A 60-million-year-old snake fossil found in South America measured about 50 feet (15 m).

Fossils and skeletons have helped scientists learn about pythons and their ancestors.

Pythons and Boas

Pythons are closely related to a family of snakes known as boa constrictors. However, boas and pythons are not the same. One important difference is that pythons lay eggs that later hatch. In contrast, boas give birth to live baby snakes. Boas are generally smaller than pythons. The largest boa species grow to be about 13 feet (4 m) long. Boas are often found in parts of North America, Central America, and South America, as well as on Caribbean islands.

Boas and pythons are similar in many ways, though. They both have flexible jaws that grow wide for eating large prey. Both types of snake usually hide and then attack their prey by surprise. Many boa species also have the heat-sensing pit organs that most pythons have.

FUN FACT! Some python species can hold their breath for up to 30 minutes at a time.

Boas can be hard to tell apart from their python relatives.

CHAPTER 5

Pythons Today

Humans have long been drawn to pythons. They are fascinated by the snakes' size and strength. Because most pythons are peaceful and not harmful to humans, many people choose to adopt them as pets. Some python owners are responsible and well prepared. However, many are not.

People often adopt young pythons. These pythons need more and more space as they grow. They are also very good at escaping from their tanks. As the baby pythons become adults, they also need more food. This can quickly become more expensive than their owners had planned.

Frustrated python owners often try to get rid of their unwanted pets by setting them free in the wild. When owners place their pythons into a new habitat, it throws the ecosystem out of balance. Pythons become an invasive species.

Python owners must learn a lot about their pets to raise them safely and responsibly.

Pythons in the Everglades

The Everglades is an area in Florida that has been invaded by Burmese pythons and African rock pythons. Officials believe that many pet owners dumped these snakes into the Everglades when they couldn't care for them. It is also possible that some pythons escaped during hurricanes when pet shops and breeding areas were damaged.

Now the pythons are threatening ecosystems in the Everglades because there are no animals in Florida that can help control the python population. Because pythons can lay dozens of eggs at a time, the number of snakes is growing quickly. The pythons compete for food with Florida's **native** snake species. With less food for the native snakes, they could become **endangered**.

FUN FACT! Experts estimate that there are somewhere between 30,000 and 100,000 invasive pythons living in southern Florida.

Florida officials work to remove invasive pythons from the wild.

Pythons in Danger

Throughout the world, pythons are losing their natural habitats. This happens when natural areas are destroyed as new roads and homes are built. Trees are knocked down, woodlands are paved over, and bodies of water are filled in with dirt. When pythons are forced from their normal surroundings, they head for villages, cities, and other areas where people live. This frightens humans. It also puts pets and other small animals in danger.

In addition, many pythons are still hunted throughout the world. People kill the snakes for their beautiful skins. The skins are used to make pants, purses, shoes, and other items. In China, python skin is used to make a musical instrument called the erhu. It is said that python skin gives the erhu its unique sound.

The interesting designs on python skins make the snakes popular targets for hunters.

Protecting Pythons

Indian pythons are on the international endangered species list. They could die out completely if they are not protected. Other species of pythons are on the threatened list. This means that people must take action so they do not become endangered.

To protect pythons, some governments have passed laws. Conservation laws preserve pythons' habitats. Countries with these laws will not easily be able to clear natural areas for lumber or farmland. Other countries have laws that prevent the killing and selling of pythons for their skins, which are then used to make shoes, belts, and handbags.

Zoos are also committed to saving pythons. Some zoos refuse to accept pythons that have been caught in the wild. And zoos help educate people about pythons so they no longer fear these strong, beautiful reptiles. As more people work together to save the python, we can look forward to a future where these amazing animals are no longer threatened.

Zoos care for pythons and help educate the public about these remarkable creatures.

Words to Know

brumation (broo-MAY-shuhn) — a process where reptiles become less active during the colder months to conserve energy

clutch (KLUHCH) — a nest of eggs

cold-blooded (KOHLD BLUHD-id) — having a body temperature that changes according to the temperature of the surroundings

conservation (kon-sur-VAY-shuhn) — the act of protecting an environment and the living things in it

constrictors (kuhn-STRIK-turz) — snakes that kill prey by squeezing it to death

digest (dye-JEST) — to break down food in the organs of digestion so that it can be absorbed into the blood and used by the body

dilate (DYE-layt) — to become wide

ecosystem (EE-koh-sis-tuhm) — all the living things in a place and their relation to the environment

endangered (en-DAYN-jurd) — at risk of becoming extinct, usually because of human activity

fossils (FOSS-uhlz) — the hardened remains of prehistoric plants and animals

habitat (HAB-uh-tat) — the place where an animal or a plant is usually found

hibernate (HYE-bur-nate) — to sleep through the winter to survive when temperatures are cold and food is hard to find

invasive (in-VAY-siv) — describing a plant or animal that is introduced to a new habitat and may cause that habitat harm

mating (MAYT-ing) — joining together to produce babies

native (NAY-tiv) — naturally belonging to a certain place

pit organs (PIT OR-guhnz) — body parts that allow snakes to sense the temperature of objects or animals around them

predators (PREH-duh-turz) — animals that live by hunting other animals for food

prehensile (pree-HEN-sile) — able to grab or wrap around

prey (PRAY) — an animal that's hunted by another animal for food

reticulated (rih-TIK-yuh-late-id) — describing something that has a pattern that looks like a net

savannas (suh-VAN-uhz) — flat, grassy plains with few or no trees

solitary (SOL-ih-tehr-ee) — preferring to live alone

species (SPEE-sheez) — one of the groups into which animals and plants of the same genus are divided

suffocation (suhf-uh-KAY-shuhn) — the act of dying from being unable to breathe

vertebrae (VUR-tuh-bray) — small bones that make up the backbone of an animal

NORTH

AMERICA

PACIFIC

ATLANTIC

OCEAN

SOUTH
AMERICA

Python Range

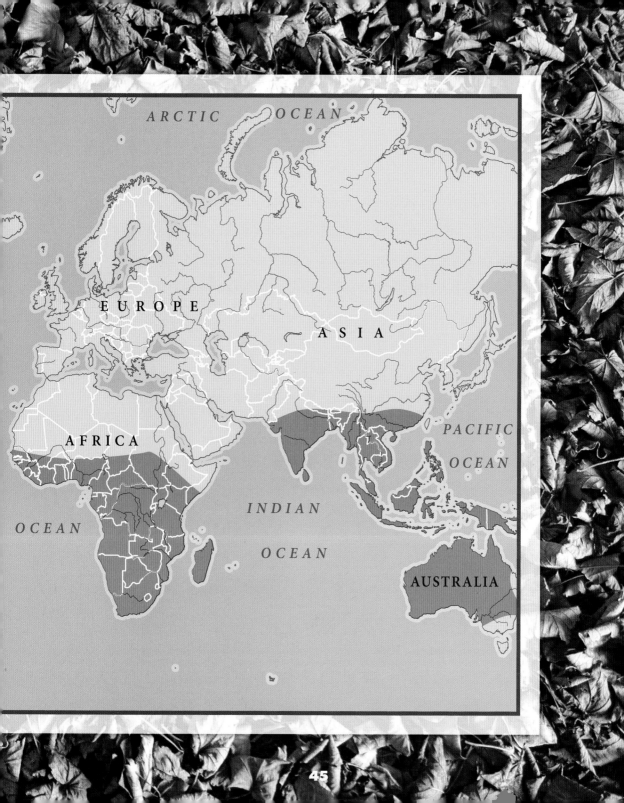

ARCTIC OCEAN

EUROPE

ASIA

AFRICA

PACIFIC OCEAN

OCEAN

INDIAN

OCEAN

AUSTRALIA

Find Out More

Books

Allyn, Daisy. *Python*. New York: Gareth Stevens Publishing, 2011.

Corwin, Jeff. *The Extraordinary Everglades*. New York: Grosset & Dunlap, 2010.

Rothaus, Don. *Pythons*. Chanhassen, MI: The Child's World, 2007.

Somervill, Barbara A. *Python*. Ann Arbor, MI: Cherry Lake Publishing, 2010.

Taylor, Barbara. *100 Things You Should Know About Snakes*. Broomall, PA: Mason Crest, 2011.

Visit this Scholastic Web site for more information on pythons:
www.factsfornow.scholastic.com
Enter the keyword **pythons**

Index

About the Author

Lucia Raatma earned a bachelor's degree from the University of South Carolina and a master's degree from New York University. She has authored dozens of books for young readers, and she particularly enjoys writing about wildlife and conservation. She and her family often visit a Burmese python at their local zoo.